PMT CRAZE

GW00891732

TOUCH ME AND I'LL KILL YOU

by **JAN KING**

Illustrated by
DON SMITH

PUBLISHED BY

POWERFRESH
NORTHAMPTON · ENGLAND

UNDER LICENSE FROM CCC PUBLICATIONS · LOS ANGELES · USA

Published in the UK by
POWERFRESH Limited
3 Gray Street
Northampton
NN1 3QQ

Telephone 44 01604 30996
Facsimile 44 01604 21013

Cover and interior illustration by Don Smith

Cover and interior layout by Powerfresh

PMT CRAZED - TOUCH ME AND I'LL KILL YOU!
ISBN 1 874125 325

Printed in the UK by Avalon Print Northampton
        Powerfresh December 1994

INTRODUCTION

Why is it that every time a woman gets in a bad mood, men accuse her of being a bitch with PMT? Well, if these same men had to sit on a sanitary pad the size of a 747 flotation device every month for a week, go through labour and delivery, have an episiotomy, and suffer through hot flushes for five years, they would be suicidal—at best.

After enduring a lifelong battle with women's' hormonal miseries, we have the right to act bitchy! And "PMT: Touch Me And I'll Kill You" will recount with great humour the events that make us less than delightful 30 days a month!!

PMT: License To Kill

This syndrome is viewed by men as a giant conspiracy amongst women. They think it's just a big hoax that women are using to justify being bitches. When we tell them that PMT makes us weepy, irritable, and slightly irrational, they refuse to take us seriously.

Well, they better wake up and smell the gunpowder burns. Women are now using PMT in the courtroom as a defence for justifiable homicide and getting away with murder!! So guys, you'd better hide your wife's nail files, ice picks, and under wire bras for 20 days a month if you know what's good for you.

PMT: The Psychic Network

Q: Do you know what they call a woman who has PMT and ESP?

A: A BITCH who knows EVERYTHING.

MENSTRUAL MISERY: The Hormonally Challenged

Women are getting pretty sick of the menstrual thing. And we're holding our hormones accountable. For two weeks we're PRE-MENSTRUAL, then for one week we're MENSTRUAL, and for the other two weeks we're POST-MENSTRUAL.

Hell—if we get <u>five good minutes</u> a month, it's a miracle!

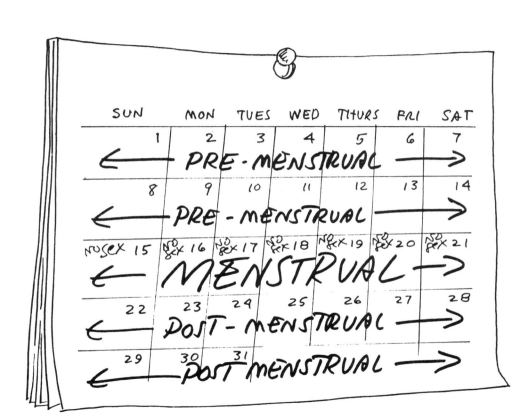

I HATE MY PERIOD—Period!

You can always count on getting your period when you are:

· In a restaurant wearing your best WHITE dress.

· On your honeymoon. (Your Dad prayed very hard for it to happen this way)

· On Holiday. Pack a Designer suitcase full of tampons.

· On an airplane. The sanitary pads in the toilets are as big as a 747 and come with their own installation crew.

· Any time you are NOT carrying a tampon in your purse. Next time, listen to the advert and "don't leave home without it."

HORMONE THERAPY: Can Be Hazardous To Your Sex Life

Recently, doctors have been prescribing a drug containing the male hormone testosterone to alleviate the side effects from heavy menstrual cycles. But little has been reported about it's WORST side effect: heart attack— of the shocked husband who wakes up one morning next to his wife who is sporting a bushy mustache and an advanced case of 5 O'clock shadow.

THE GYNAECOLOGY EXAMINATION: Taking A Deeper Look

No wonder we're fed up... first, we are asked to lie down on a steel examination table in a room whose temperature has never been above 32 degrees F. Then we are supposed to cover our naked bodies with the 4" x 4" sheet supplied.

However, this actually works to our advantage in the end (pun intended), because a frozen vaginal canal makes for a much less painful examination.

GYNAECOLOGY EXAMINATION II: Show and Tell

So here you are lying with your legs spread in different time zones, when the doctor comes in followed by a line of pimply-faced, Medical Students.

They are all most anxious to get a peek at your innermost organs and proceed to fanatically write down their comments. The only thing more humiliating would be to see this event featured on "Kilroy" the next day.

THE MAMMOGRAM: Chernobyl Revisited

This so-called "safe" procedure employs a machine with the nuclear potential of creating another Chernobyl aimed directly at your shivering breasts.

Then a flat plate comes down and squashes one breast at a time into the shape and consistency of a fried egg. You are told to hold your breath for a few seconds during the actual X-Ray. But your breasts are being squashed so hard, there isn't ANY air left in your body after letting out that one long scream.

SEX DURING PREGNANCY: Fantasy Island

Tips on how to spice up your sex life during pregnancy:

· The wife should not attempt getting on top during the last three months of pregnancy... unless the husband is proficient in bench pressing Chieftain tanks.

· Be inventive. Try role playing to inject excitement into your sex lives. "Captain Ahab harpoons Moby Dick" or "Sir Edmund Hilary conquers Mt. Everest" are two popular favourites.

· Enlist the aid of sexual fantasy. You pretend he's Mel Gibson, and he pretends you're NOT PREGNANT.

A WOMAN IS HER MOST BEAUTIFUL DURING PREGNANCY: The Big Lie

This statement is made by people in need of an optician. The truth is that pregnancy causes the following changes which you'll be forced to endure:

· HAIR- you'll grow a fuzzy little black line of hair that makes a track from your belly-button downwards. And how about that hormonal moustache?

· STRETCH MARKS- that look like runs in double-knit polyester stockings. They will have the same depth and tread as a new set of Goodyears.

· ENGORGED BREASTS- when you take off your 42Z bra at night, those giant boobs will feel like two hot heifers plopping on your belly.

· VARICOSE VEINS- they look like Macaroni and are going to require double strength Queen Size support stockings—i.e. big enough for a 300 pound "Drag Queen."

Biggest Lie On The Planet: A Woman Is   At Her Most Beautiful Time During Pregnancy

MORNING SICKNESS: Scarf and Barf

If ONLY it was confined to the mornings! By the second month of pregnancy, the carpet between your bed and the bathroom will have skid marks rivalling those at a Silverstone grand prix. In your hormonally altered state, ordinary smells become enemy stimuli causing you to throw up your dinner at any given second.

It can be especially distressing when you sit down to dinner at your in-laws, take one bite of your mother-in-law's prized beef stroganoff, and promptly hurl it all over her priceless lace tablecloth.

NATURAL CHILDBIRTH: A Pain In The Butt

The biggest piece of B.S. ever uttered:

"Natural childbirth is the most BEAUTIFUL experience a woman will ever have."

The Truth:

"Natural childbirth is spelled A-G-O-N-Y."

LABOUR: Paying Your Dues

HOW WILL I KNOW WHEN IT'S TIME TO GO TO THE HOSPITAL ONCE LABOUR HAS STARTED?

· When your "persistent indigestion" is accompanied by contractions every three minutes.

· Go immediately to the hospital when your contractions are severely interfering with your foreplay. Do not get dressed and do not stay to collect your £200.

· When your favourite pair of trainers are doubling as flotation devices.

· When you look down at your shoes and see an extra pair of feet dangling between your own.

LABOUR and DELIVERY: Fatal Contraction

The act of "pushing" in labour is an entirely primal experience. It can only be described as feeling like you are trying to expel the Manchester United football team.

And when you're half dead from exhaustion, the doctor will tell you NOT to push anymore. This is like trying to hold back the contents of the Hoover Dam.

SEX AFTER PREGNANCY: Future Shock

This can be a very "touchy" issue. Those stretched, cut, and stitched areas are going to be mighty tender for a while. But your husband is going to be "rarin' to go" after his enforced celibacy. So here are a few suggestions on when it's best to resume sex:

· It would be best to wait at least until you get back to the recovery room.

· When the doctor has removed your 235 episiotomy stitches OR six months...whichever comes LAST.

· Before you do it for the first time after delivering, load up on Codeine and Valium. Then try to stay awake long enough to make it through the usual two minutes of foreplay.

HEY, SWEETIE, COULD YOU MAKE IT SNAPPY? IF IT TAKES MUCH LONGER I'M GONNA BE OUT OF THE MOOD.

SEX AFTER PREGNANCY II: Mission Impossible

Here are some "classic" excuses to give your husband in response to his requests for sex right after the baby comes:

· "Not tonight, dear. My hormones are killing me."

· "Just a minute, sweetie. I have to finish expressing my last eight gallons of breast milk."

· "Would you mind starting without me for the next few weeks?"

· "Well, if you think I'm strong enough...okay. But I can't keep the oxygen mask off for too long."

· "Okay, darling. But remember that my 300 razor sharp steel episiotomy sutures haven't been removed yet."

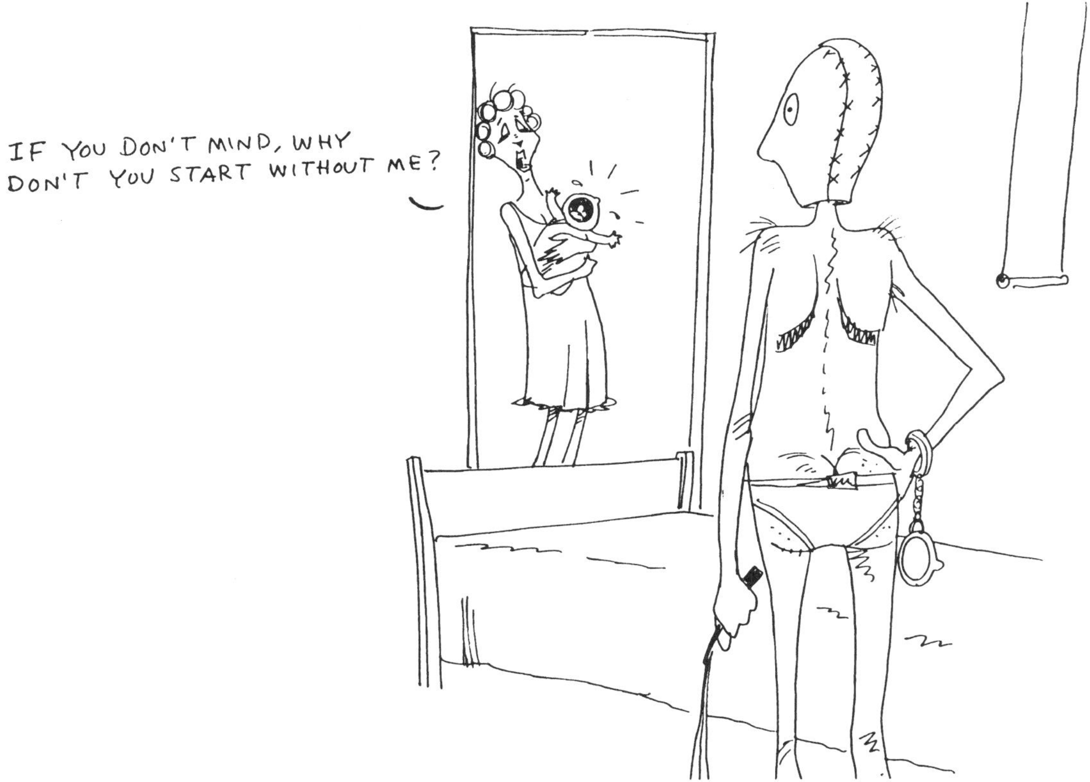
IF YOU DON'T MIND, WHY DON'T YOU START WITHOUT ME?

COSMETIC SURGERY: The Face Of Things To Come

In order to keep our men interested, we have to always show our "best face." And when the only face you've got is not what he considers even passable anymore, we head for the nearest plastic surgeon.

Be prepared to pay with CASH ONLY. And be careful never to utter words like "BUPA" or "health insurance"—it makes their hands shake.

Ever resourceful, the plastic surgeons carefully drop these "buzz words" to make sure their insecure patients are never offended:

PHRASE	TRANSLATION
redundant skin	wrinkled old hag
mild swelling	a head that looks like Humpty Dumpty
some discomfort	same pain as going 15 rounds with Tyson

THE PENCIL TEST: Measuring Your Breast I.Q

To determine if your aging breasts are losing their firmness, place a pencil under one of them. If it falls out, it means that your breast tissue is still firm and youthful.

However, if you keep shoving pencils in there and none of them fall out, it's time to ask yourself a few hard questions. And once you pass 100, emergency plastic surgery will be your only answer.

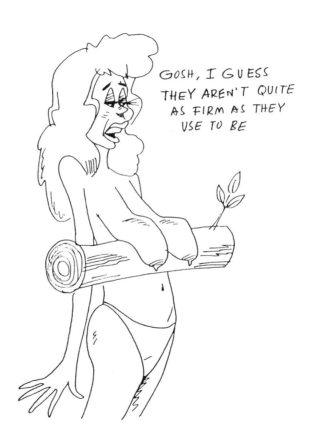

THE BOOB JOB: The Bigger The Better

The biggest joke in the world is when a woman says she wants to get her breasts enlarged only to "please herself." Nothing could be more obvious than the one and only reason women get boob jobs—men LOVE big breasts!! Yes, big breasts mean POWER!.

And as far as all men are concerned, the bigger the better. If men were given the option of having the organ of their choice enlarged, they would all look like they had a giant Xmas tree in their pants.

THE BOOB JOB II: More Bounce Per Ounce

Having big breasts will give you a new slant on life—literally. Besides listing forward at a 35 degree angle, you'll find that you're the life of the party by delighting friends and family with an array of stunts you only dared fantasise about before:

· floating in a hot tub without sinking

· balancing two martini glasses on both boobs

· lying on your back without having your boobs disappear into your armpits

· doing the tango with a short guy and knocking him out on the turns

HYSTERECTOMY: The Cutting Edge

This operation is now considered one of the most frequently performed of all "unnecessary surgeries." Are doctors' just out for the money? To answer this question, a woman must be very knowledgeable about her own body. And to identify the "knife happy" surgeons, be on the lookout for those who insist a hysterectomy is medically indicated:

· While you're still on the table, after delivering your first child.

· As a 40th birthday present to yourself.

· The week before their malpractice insurance bill is due.

· To fill up his morning's surgical schedule.

HYSTERECTOMY MYTHS: Cutting Through It

These myths about hysterectomy need to be debunked as purely old wives tales:

· "After a hysterectomy I'll only be half a woman."
-FALSE. You'll be 2/3 to 3/4 depending on how much was removed.

· "Sex won't be the same after the operation."
-NONSENSE. It will continue to be every bit as dull and boring as before.

· "I'll be filled with remorse after I do it."
-NO WAY. You'll be filled with WIND—and enough to launch the Goodyear Blimp.

· "I will lose my driving urge for sex."
-NOT EXACTLY. Your preference will simply switch to the BACK SEAT.

· "Losing my female organs will be a constant reminder that I'm hollow inside."
-UNTRUE. You'll only echo if somebody shouts directly into your cervix.

CONTRACEPTION: Taking The Right Position

THE DIAPHRAGM

The things we have to go through for men!! Ugh! Inserting one of these babies properly requires the dexterity of a seasoned magician like David Copperfield. You might want to ask David to do it for you, but chances are he's busy with Claudia's.

Constructed of latex rubber with a spring action stronger than a mousetraps', extreme caution must be taken when trying to position it in the vaginal canal. Letting it slip before it's half-way in could result in the diaphragm shooting across the room and taking out your cat. When you feel it hit the tip of the cervix (you're in up to your elbow by now), let the spring go, allowing it to snap into place. Brace yourself, because your uterus will be absorbing shock waves of an intensity not felt since Hiroshima.

The Diaphragm

CONTRACEPTION II: Don't Get Soaked

THE SPONGE

It is small, compact, and manufactured by the O-Cello company. Touted as safe and effective, it does have one side effect. Once it's in place, the wearer is cautioned not to go swimming for risk of draining the pool.

Also, head injury is another possible side effect. Carelessly flopping into a chair might create a "rebound" effect, catapulting one upward into the ceiling.

Contraceptive Sponge

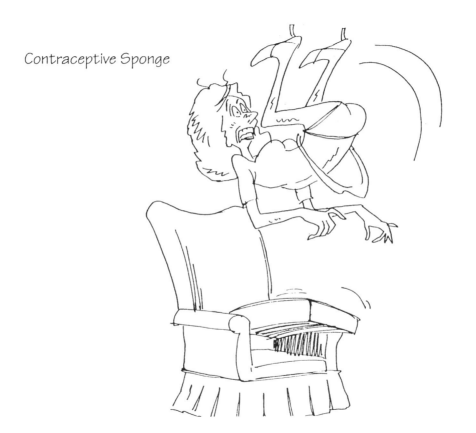

CONTRACEPTION III:
Plop, Plop, Fizz, Fizz... This Is What Protection Is

FOAM

In order to be effective, contraceptive foam has to be used in the same quantities it takes to land a crippled 747 on a runway. Another drawback is that bathing is prohibited for 24 hours after application, because the user now has the dangerous potential of acting as a giant-sized Alka-Seltzer tablet.

Contraceptive Foam

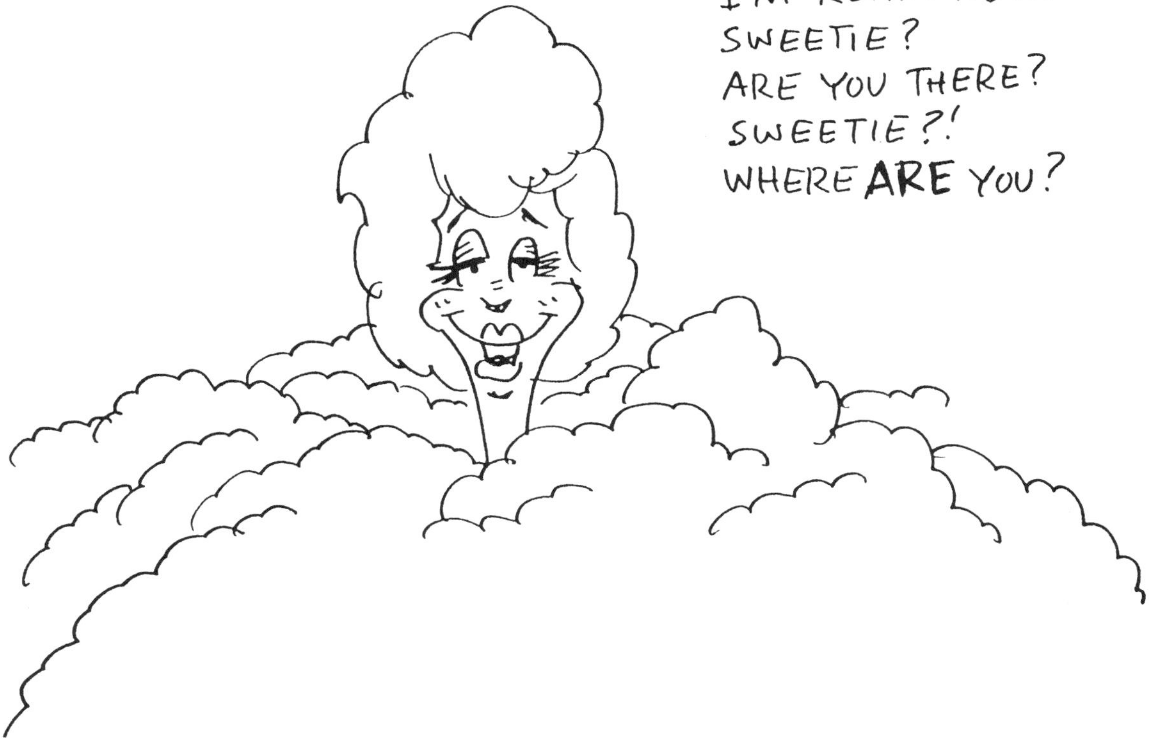

CONTRACEPTION IV: A Bitter Pill To Swallow

THE PILL

Who needs it? The package alone contains more warnings than you would find on a nuclear missile. Some of the possible side effects include:

· stroke

· heart attack

· cancer

· high cholesterol

Plus if you smoke, the incidence is doubled. If you smoke AND drink—triple it. And if you smoke, drink, AND have sex—forget it!! You won't live long enough to finish out the package. Expert medical advice tells us that Russian Roulette gives BETTER ODDS.

The Pill

CONTRACEPTION V: The Great Condom Caper

CONDOMS

Most women wish that manufacturers would design a package that takes less time to open. While all men still cling to the story that they can "last the whole evening," in reality, most of them can't last until the seal is broken.

The second complaint is from the men themselves, who are concerned about the expiration date stamped on a box of condoms. They all say the same thing:

"Who needs this kind of pressure?"

FOREPLAY AFTER 40: Energy Conservation

Do you remember it? He probably doesn't. Past 40, there is very little actual kissing going on in the bedroom. It takes too much time and saps too much of the energy necessary to complete the actual act. A common practice past 40 is for both partners to meet in the centre of the bed, shake hands, and get on with it.

Younger women spend all their time worrying about whether they're having the "right" kind of orgasm or not. There is the vaginal, the clitoral, the multiple, and the most popular—the FAKED. But today's women aren't worried so much about multiple orgasms, they're worried about multiple ORGANISMS.

SEX AFTER 40: Coming Out On Top

After 40, a woman's main concern during sex is to display her body in the most flattering position possible. This automatically eliminates you from ever being on top again during lovemaking, because you'll look like somebody LET THE AIR OUT OF YOUR FACE.

Sex After 40 — Never Get On Top. It looks like the air came out of your face.

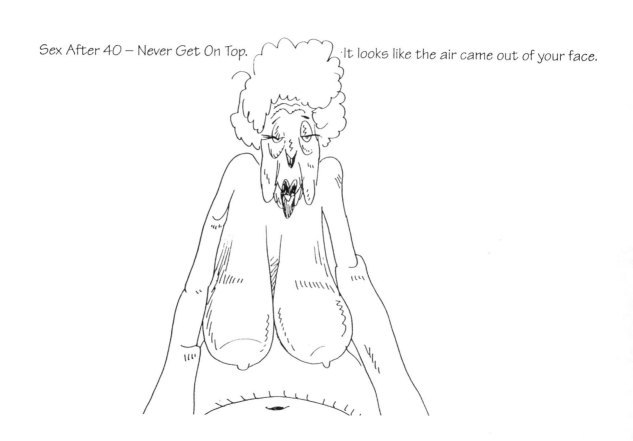

SEX AFTER 40 II: Who Turned Out The Lights?

LIGHTING

The older we get, the more we've got to hide. In your 20's, you made love in broad daylight on the beach, in the car, and in the shower. But after 40, we're trying to hide a lot more than just our crow's feet. Our bedroom will slowly make the transition from a 60 watt flood bulb, to a 40 watt, to a night light, then to half a candlepower generated by an elderly firefly.

By age 50, we're talking about a room so dark it can only be navigated by bats.

CONCLUSION

There—now don't you feel better? It's like one big group therapy session, getting our hormonal problems out into the open and laughing at them.

At least we've reached an age when it's finally okay to discuss these topics publicly. At one time it was considered "disgusting" to even talk about your period. Now in the light of topics like Bosnia, the Yorkshire Ripper, and the Hungerford massacre,
a little menstrual bloodshed is like a drop in the bucket.

TITLES BY
POWERFRESH

CRINKLED 'N' WRINKLED
DRIVEN CRAZY
OH NO ITS XMAS AGAIN
TRUE LOVE
IT'S A BOY
IT'S A GIRL
NOW WE ARE 40
FUNNY SIDE OF 40 HIM
FUNNY SIDE OF 40 HER
FUNNY SIDE OF 50 HIM
FUNNY SIDE OF 50 HER
FUNNY SIDE OF GOLF
FUNNY SIDE OF 60'S
FUNNY SIDE OF SEX
GERRY ATRIC'S GAG BOOK
THE COMPLETE WIMPS GUIDE TO SEX
THE COMPLETE BASTARDS GUIDE TO BUSINESS SURVIVAL
THE COMPLETE BASTARDS GUIDE TO SPORT
THE COMPLETE BASTARDS GUIDE TO GOLF
THE COMPLETE BASTARDS GUIDE TO LIFE
THE COMPLETE BASTARDS GUIDE TO SEX
MALCOM
KEEP FIT WITH YOUR CAT
THE OFFICE FROM HELL
MONSTERS
MARITAL BLISS AND OTHER OXYMORONS
THE ART OF SLOBOLOGY
IT'S NO FUN BEING A MOTHER
THE DEFINITIVE GUIDE TO VASECTOMY
PMT CRAZED

ALL TITLES RETAIL AT   £2.99